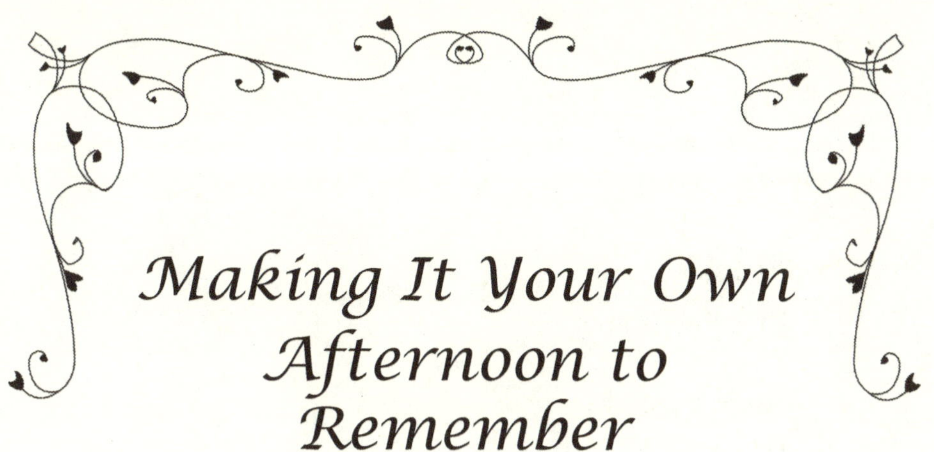

Making It Your Own Afternoon to Remember

by

Amy Lawrence

Published by:

ATR Publishing

Cover Photo by:

Amy Lawrence

Back Cover Photo by:

Sirlin Photographers

(916)444-8464

http://www.sirlin.com/

ISBN: 978-0-9796170-2-7

An Afternoon to Remember is dedicated to educating others in the art of taking tea. Our mission is to provide a unique upscale experience where customers are pampered and can relax, socialize and celebrate special occasions while enjoying excellent teas and delectable treats. Tea rooms entice you to sit leisurely, and this is the main goal and purpose of our tea room making your experience here truly...

"An Afternoon to Remember."

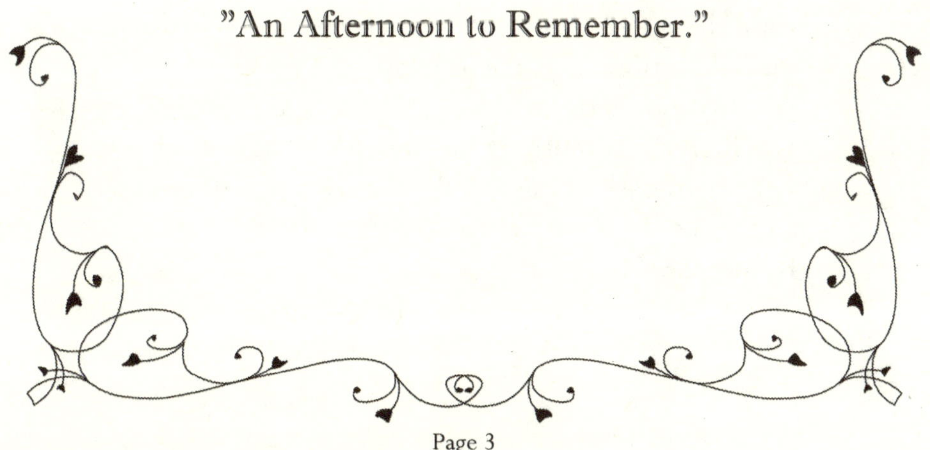

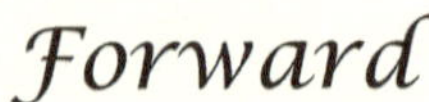

Forward

I've thought long and hard over the title of my third cookbook. We've had so many questions over the last 2 years about recipes, ingredients and how-to's. People always wonder where we get our recipes. Some recipes come from my wonderful staff and their own recipe collections, some of them are handed down from family members, and many are adaptations of recipes we have tasted or have wanted to try. Some are even recipes we have created in a pinch with the ingredients on hand. With every recipe, however, we add our own flair. So when you make these recipes, keep that in mind.

Our recipes are not "Step-by-Step". The measurements given are not exact measurements, we make everything according to taste. If you love garlic, add tons of it, if you don't like olives, then leave them out and add something else. Feel free to experiment. What's the worst thing that could happen? You have to throw it out and start again. Chances are though, you'll create something new and delicious. Find your own dash of flair, add your own signature and make it your own, "Afternoon to Remember".

Dedication

I would like to dedicate this cookbook to my two wonderful cooks. Without them, there would be no cookbook. In the beginning I played a huge part in the cooking. Now I just make scones and quiche. It was a godsend when Connie came along. At first it was so hard for me to let someone else do the cooking. I was so particular and I didn't think anyone could live up to my expectations, but Connie did and she did it even better. She is our dessert queen. When we added Carla to our staff, she became the sandwich queen. Most of the sandwich recipes in this cookbook were created by her. She has a great flair for seasoning. The two of them together make a dynamite pair.

I have a wonderful staff. Every single one of them brings a unique quality and charm to our tearoom. They are all so dedicated. They work long hours especially during the Anniversary party and the holiday season. They come in on their days off to help, take home laundry, do the shopping, even babysit on occasion. They are my family. I would like to thank each and every one of them.

As many of you know we are losing a few this year to pursue other dreams. Tessa, my right hand, will be going off to college. It's hard to

Dedication Continued

imagine the tearoom without her. She has been here from almost the very beginning. Keri is also going off to college. We were so fortunate to have her twice. Chelsea has moved from our kitchen to culinary school in Napa. Even though I will miss them, I wish them all the best. I know they will go on to do great things.

I would also like to thank my family. Although it's getting easier, I still work long hours at times. My husband is always there for me, he listens, guides and thankfully works from home. Without his commitment to me and our boys, I could have never started this tea room. I'm so fortunate to have him in my life. My two boys, Thomas and Jacob are my sunshines. They always bring a smile to my face with their goofy entertainment or their endearing notes of love. On occasion, they even have Oprah waiting for me when I get home from a long day with a blanket spread out on the couch. Yes, they are the joy of my life.

Last of all, I would like to thank our customers. This year we received the Tea Room Experience Digest Reader's Choice award for Best Small City Tea Room in the United States. We could have never received this award without so many votes from our loyal customers. Thank you all!

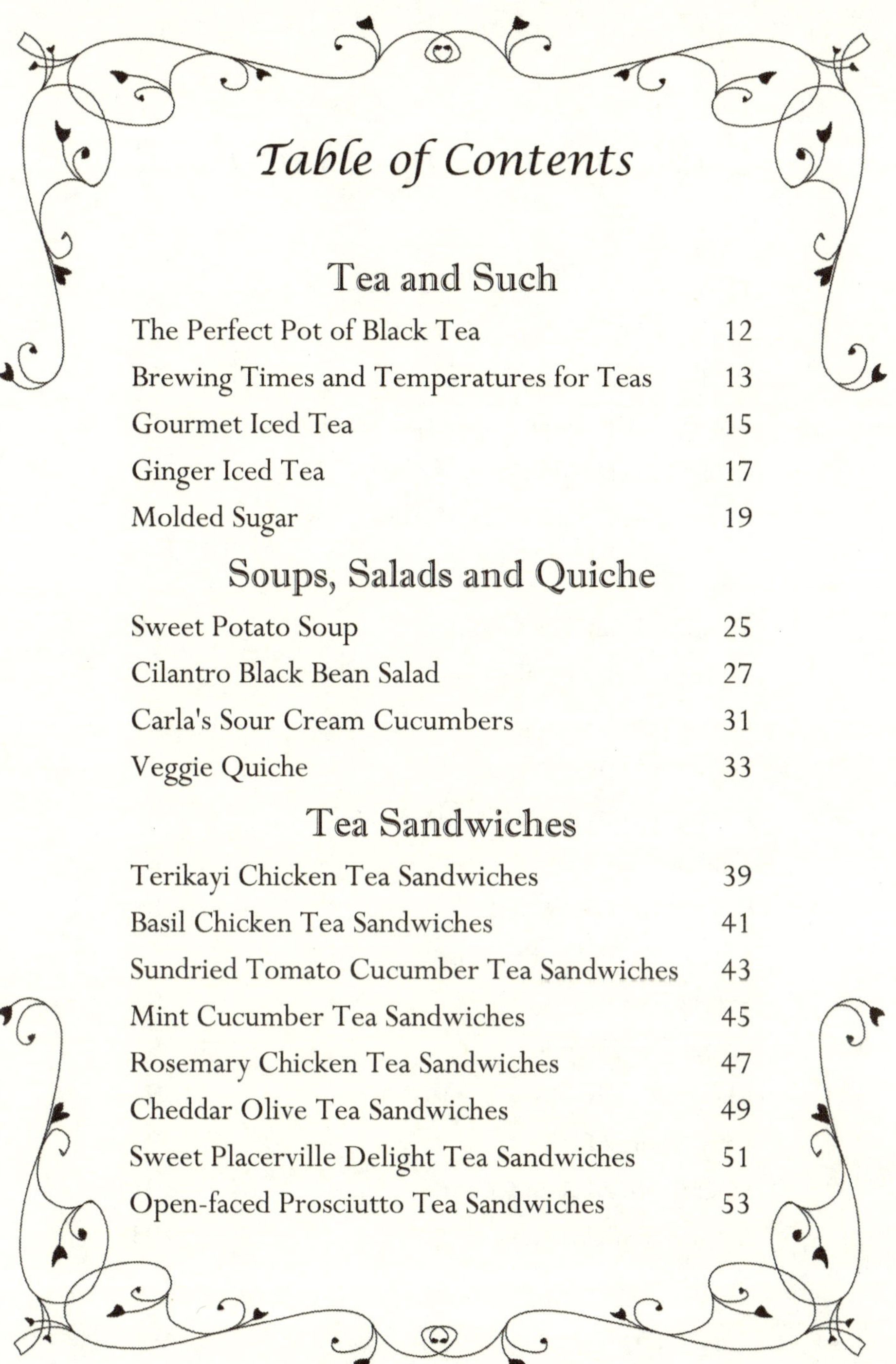

Table of Contents

Tea and Such

Soups, Salads and Quiche

Tea Sandwiches

Table of Contents Continued

Tea Sandwiches

Desserts

Table of Contents Continued

Desserts

Scones and Condiments

Tea and Such

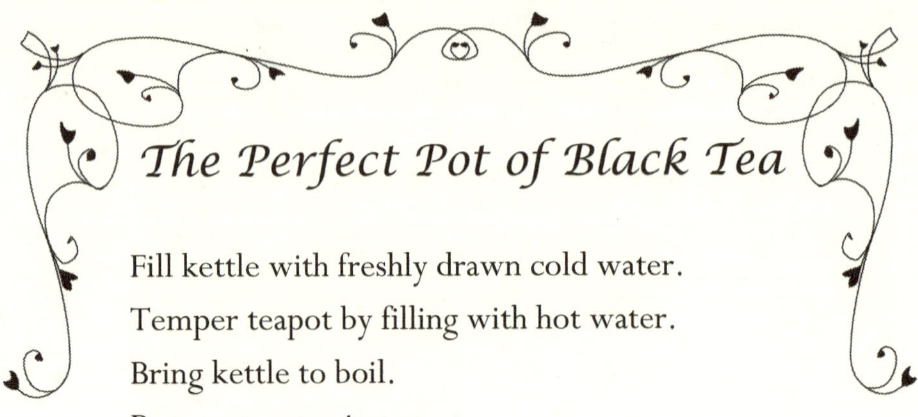

The Perfect Pot of Black Tea

Fill kettle with freshly drawn cold water.

Temper teapot by filling with hot water.

Bring kettle to boil.

Pour out water in teapot.

Place tea sock in teapot.

Add one scant teaspoon of tea per cup.

Pour boiling water over leaves.

Replace teapot lid.

Steep for 3-5 minutes for black tea.

Decant or remove tea sock with leaves.

Stir and serve.

Cover with a tea cozy or use a warmer to keep tea piping hot.

Enjoy!

Brewing Teas and Tissanes

Black Tea

Water – almost boiling
Steeping time – normally 3-4 minutes. Some Darjeelings are best at 3 minutes.

Oolongs

Water – a little less than boiling – around 195°
Steeping time – same as green teas

Green Teas

Water – hot, about 180°
Steeping time – Most green teas can be steeped more than once. If multiple infusions are desired then start with a steeping time of 2 minutes and then increase it by 1 minute for every additional infusion.

White Teas

Water – hot, about 180°
Steeping time – White teas are very mild. To get the full flavor, steep for 10-12 minutes.

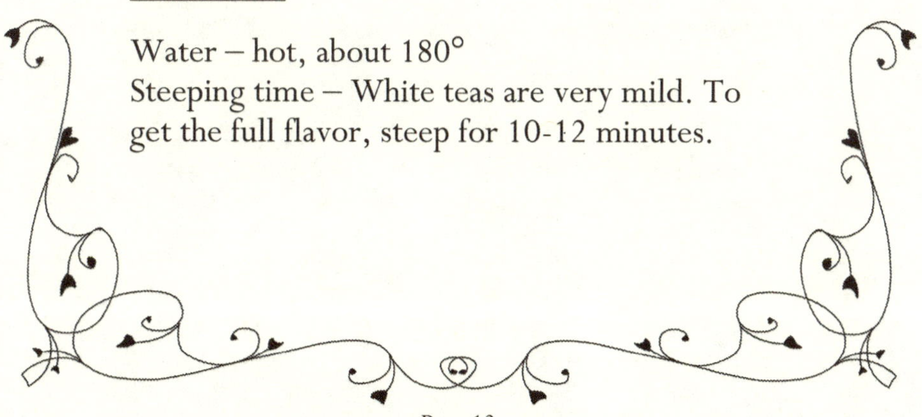

Brewing Teas and Tissanes Continued

Flavored Teas

Water – almost boiling
Steeping time – 3-4 minutes

Tissanes or Herbal Blends

Water – boiling

Steeping time – 7 minutes

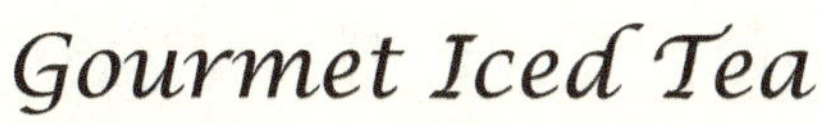

Gourmet Iced Tea

This will make approximately 2 quarts of gourmet iced tea with loose tea leaves. Use fresh, cold water from the tap or spring water. Do not reuse water you have already boiled since the oxygen will have evaporated and this affects the taste of the tea.

Measure ¼ cup of tea leaves (to make 2 quarts or 8 cups) into your infuser. For this quantity of leaves, you will need a large infuser for the leaves to have room to expand and brew properly. A cotton tea sock or the large basket infuser will work perfectly. Use a tea pot to house the infuser and brew the tea.

Heat 4 cups of water until it reaches the correct temperature: generally, steaming for green and almost a full boil for black teas, oolongs, herbal infusions and fruit blends. Pour it over the leaves immediately and cover your teapot.

Brew the tea for 5 minutes for black teas, 2-3 minutes for green and 10 minutes for Rooibos or herbal teas. Over brewing can cause the tea to taste bitter so use the appropriate time according to the specific tea.

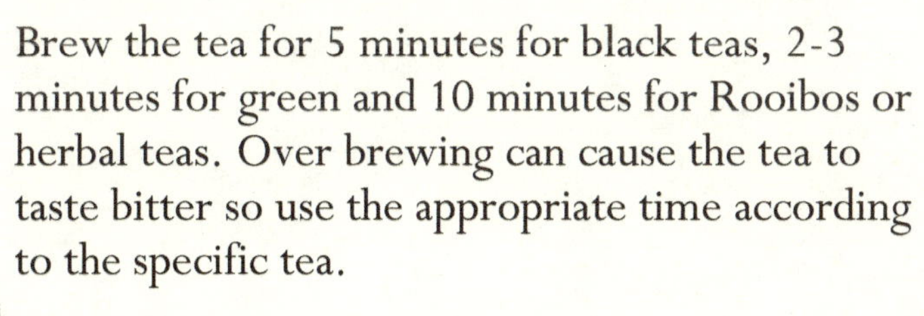

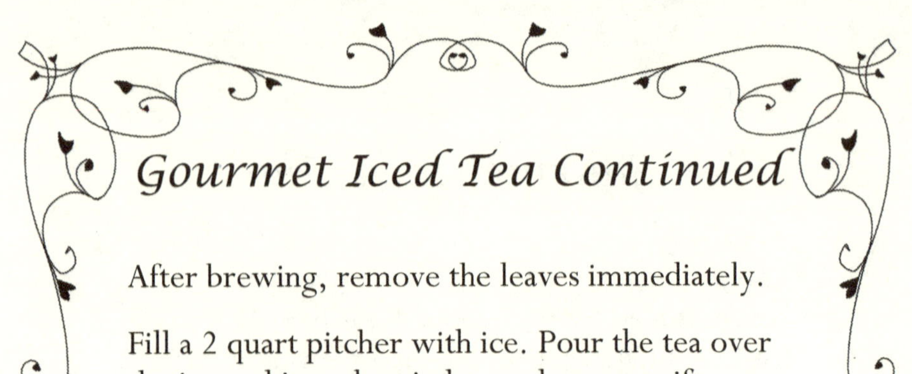

Gourmet Iced Tea Continued

After brewing, remove the leaves immediately.

Fill a 2 quart pitcher with ice. Pour the tea over the ice and into the pitcher and sweeten if desired. Then, add enough cold tap water to fill the pitcher. This will make a strong tea, you can dilute with more water according to your taste.

A 4 oz. tin makes about 14 quarts. A 2 oz. tin makes about 6 quarts. A 1 oz tin makes about 3 quarts.

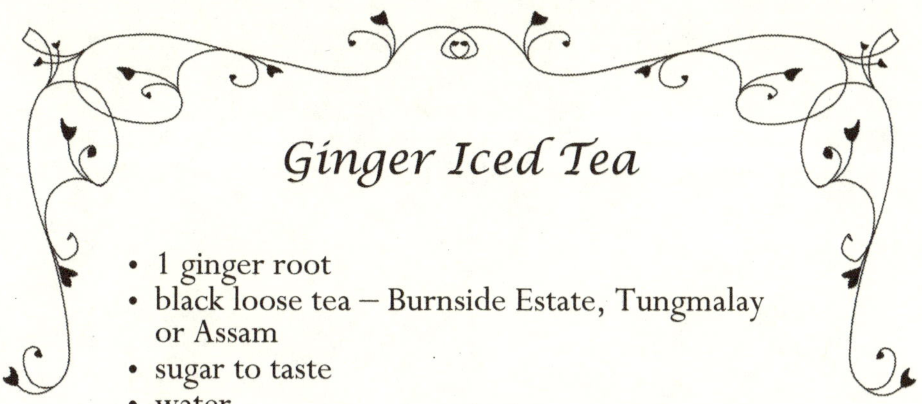

Ginger Iced Tea

- 1 ginger root
- black loose tea – Burnside Estate, Tungmalay or Assam
- sugar to taste
- water

Slice ginger root into small thin pieces. Place in a small saucepan. Add about 2 cups of water. Add sugar to taste (I use about 1 tablespoon, but I don't like my iced tea very sweet). Boil for 10 minutes, stirring occasionally. Turn heat to low and simmer for about 30 minutes. Discard ginger root.

Make iced tea according to Gourmet Iced Tea directions. Add enough of the ginger syrup to taste. I like to put the ginger syrup in a small cream pitcher and let friends add their own to taste right at the table.

Notes

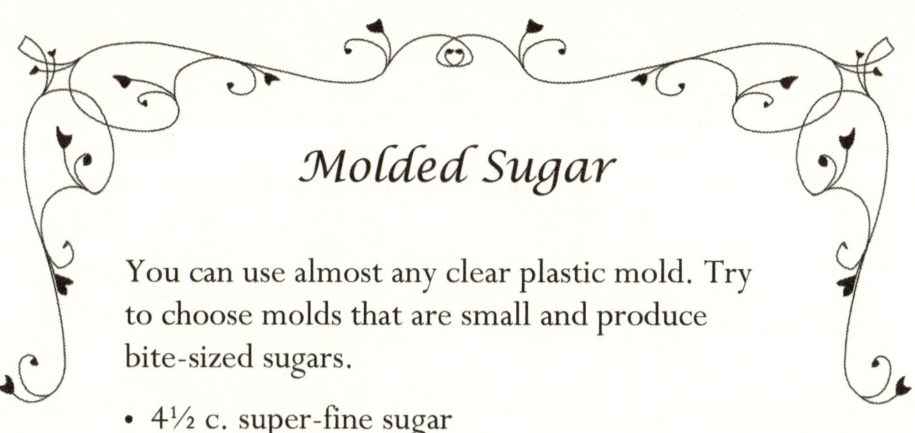

Molded Sugar

You can use almost any clear plastic mold. Try to choose molds that are small and produce bite-sized sugars.

- 4½ c. super-fine sugar
- 3 T. water
- Icing coloring. concentrated paste – we use Wilton

Measure sugar into a medium mixing bowl. In a small glass, measure 3 T. water. Dip toothpick into coloring and then dip into measured water. Stir until paste is dissolved. Just use a small amount. Pour colored water into sugar. Mix well with hands making sure all the color is evenly distributed throughout the sugar.

Pack sugar mixture into mold as firmly as possible. Press down on each figure. With a knife scrape off excess sugar back into bowl. Keep bowl covered with a wet towel as mixture dries out very quickly.

Carefully place a piece of parchment paper over mold. Place a thin sheet of cardboard on top.

Notes

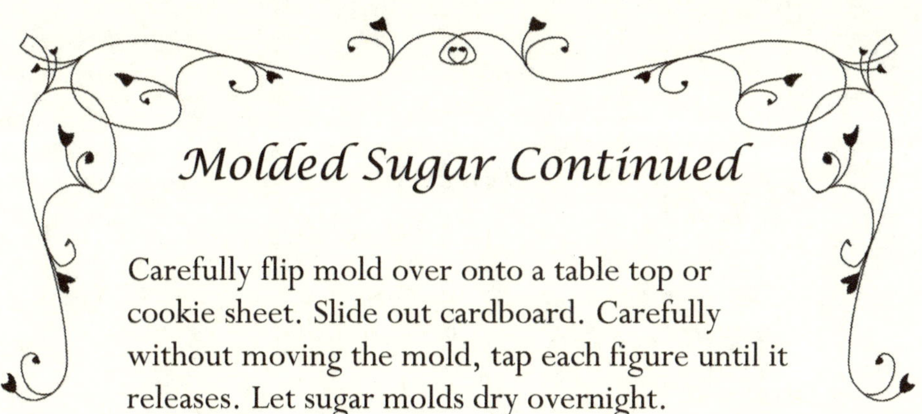

Molded Sugar Continued

Carefully flip mold over onto a table top or cookie sheet. Slide out cardboard. Carefully without moving the mold, tap each figure until it releases. Let sugar molds dry overnight.

Notes

Soups, Salads and Quiche

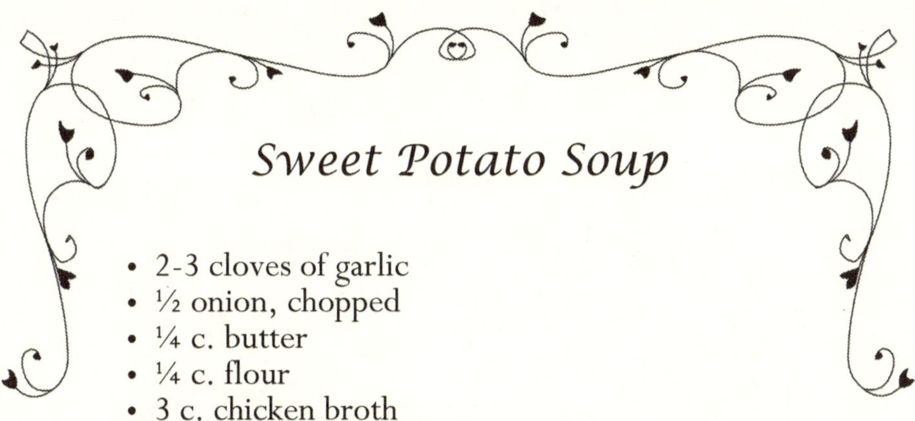

Sweet Potato Soup

- 2-3 cloves of garlic
- ½ onion, chopped
- ¼ c. butter
- ¼ c. flour
- 3 c. chicken broth
- 2 c. milk
- ½ c. whipping cream
- 5-8 sweet potatoes (depending on size)
- ¼ c. green onions – finely chopped for garnish
- 1-2 t. curry

Wash sweet potatoes. Cut off the ends and poke holes in each with a knife. Microwave for 20 minutes or until soft.

Sauté garlic, onion and butter until golden about 25 minutes. Add flour. Cook another 2 minutes. Add chicken broth, milk and cream and stir until smooth. Peel sweet potatoes and add to broth mixture. Puree mixture with an immersion blender or food processor. Add 1-2 t. curry depending on your taste. Heat mixture until warmed, but do not boil as it will curdle. Garnish with the green onion. Enjoy!

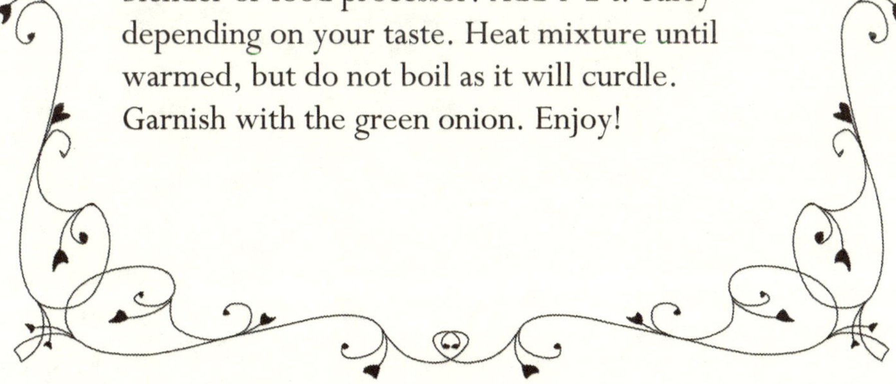

Notes

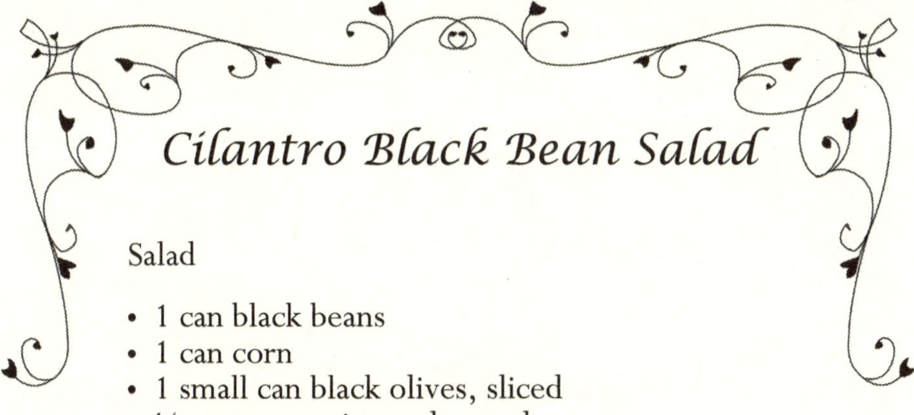

Cilantro Black Bean Salad

Salad

- 1 can black beans
- 1 can corn
- 1 small can black olives, sliced
- ½ c. green onions, chopped
- 2 small Roma tomatoes
- 1 c. cheddar cheese cut into small cubes
- 1 small bag fresh spinach finely chopped
- 1 cup pumpkin seed kernels
- cumin
- garlic salt
- seasoning salt

Dressing

- 1 t. garlic powder
- 2 garlic cloves, peeled
- ½ t. black pepper
- 1 t. seasoning salt
- 1½ c. vegetable oil
- ⅓ c. red wine vinegar
- ½ c. parmesan cheese
- 3 small bunches cilantro, chopped
- ½ c. mayonnaise
- ¼ c. water. more or less to thin dressing to desired consistency

Notes

Cilantro Black Bean Salad Continued

Preheat oven to 400°. Spray baking pan with Pam. Arrange seeds on baking pan. Spray seeds with Pam. Sprinkle cumin, garlic salt and seasoning salt over seeds. Bake for 3-5 minutes or until toasted.

To Make Dressing: Combine in a large bowl all of the dressing ingredients, except the water. Use an immersion blender or food processor and process until smooth. Add enough water to desired consistency.

To Make Salad: Mix beans, corn, olives, green onion, tomato and cheddar cheese in a large bowl. Add spinach, dressing to taste and toss. Enjoy!

Notes

Carla's Sour Cream Cucumbers

- ½ c. sour cream
- 2 T. snipped parsley
- 2 T. tarragon vinegar
- 1 T. sugar
- 1 T. snipped chives
- 3 small thinly sliced cucumbers about 3 cups
- salt and pepper to taste

Mix all ingredients except for cucumbers. Gently fold in sliced cucumbers. Cover and chill. Makes about 6 servings.

Notes

Veggie Quiche

This is our basic recipe for veggie quiche, but we make many versions of this recipe depending on what we have on hand.

- 2 c. Jarlsberg cheese – from the Newcastle Cheese Shop
- 4 eggs
- 1 c. milk
- 1 c. whipping cream
- 1 T. flour
- ½ c. red onion chopped
- 1 pkg. frozen spinach, thawed and very well drained
- ½ c. chopped marinated artichokes
- 4 T. butter
- 2 T. fresh rosemary chopped to garnish on the top
- 1 10 inch baked pie shell

Preheat oven to 325°. Sauté onion in the butter until lightly brown. Mix eggs, milk, cream and flour together in a large mixing bowl. Add in spinach, artichokes and ½ c. cheese. Sprinkle another ½ c. shredded cheese on the bottom of the baked pie shell. Add sautéed onion on top. Carefully pour mixture over onion. Sprinkle

Notes

Veggie Quiche Continued

remaining cheese on top. Sprinkle rosemary on top of cheese. Bake for 45 minutes or until completely set (some ovens may take much longer). If the cheese starts to brown too quickly before the quiche is set, cover with tented foil. Enjoy!

Notes

Tea Sandwiches

Teriyaki Chicken Tea Sandwiches

- 3 chicken breasts
- 1 c. teriyaki sauce
- 3 green onions, chopped
- 1 small can crushed pineapple, well drained
- ½ c.-1 c. mayo
- butter
- bread (potato bread, buttermilk bread, sourdough all work well)
- parsley for decoration

Marinate chicken breasts in teriyaki sauce-overnight is best. Preheat oven to 350°. Bake chicken in pan covered with foil for about 30-45 minutes or until done. Cool. Chop or pulse lightly in the food processor.

Mix together chicken, green onions, and pineapple. Add just enough mayonnaise to bind mixture together. Spread butter on bread slices. Add filling and top with second slice. Cut into desired shapes-squares, triangles, etc. Sprinkle parsley on sides for decoration.

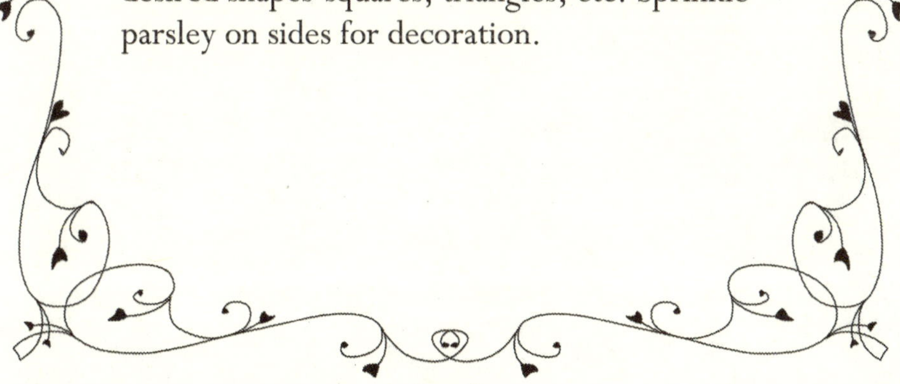

Notes

Basil Chicken Tea Sandwiches

- 2 c. cooked chicken, chopped
- ¼ c. fresh basil, chopped
- ⅓ c. pine nuts toasted
- ¼ c. parmesan cheese, shredded
- 3 green onions chopped (use white and green parts)
- ⅓ c. black olives, sliced
- 1 c. mayonnaise
- butter
- bread (potato bread, buttermilk bread, sourdough all work well)
- parsley mixed with 2 T. parmesan for decoration

Mix together first six ingredients. Add just enough mayonnaise to bind mixture together – about 1 c. Spread butter on bread slices. Add filling and top with second slice. Cut into desired shapes-squares, triangles, etc. Sprinkle parsley mixed with parmesan cheese on sides for decoration.

Notes

Carla's Sun-Dried Tomato Cucumber Tea Sandwiches

- 1½ c sun-dried tomatoes, chopped
- ½ c. parmesan cheese
- 3 cloves of garlic
- 1 t. olive oil
- ¼ c. fresh oregano
- 1 t. dried oregano
- 1 8 oz. pkg. cream cheese, softened
- ½ c. sour cream
- 2 cucumbers
- 1 loaf of dark rye
- seasoning salt and pepper to taste
- butter

Beat cream cheese until smooth. Add all ingredients except for cucumbers and seasoning salt. Butter 1 slice of bread. Spread cream cheese mixture on slice. Chill before cutting. Cut each slice into four squares. Top with a cucumber slice. Sprinkle with pepper if desired. Makes about 32 tea sandwiches.

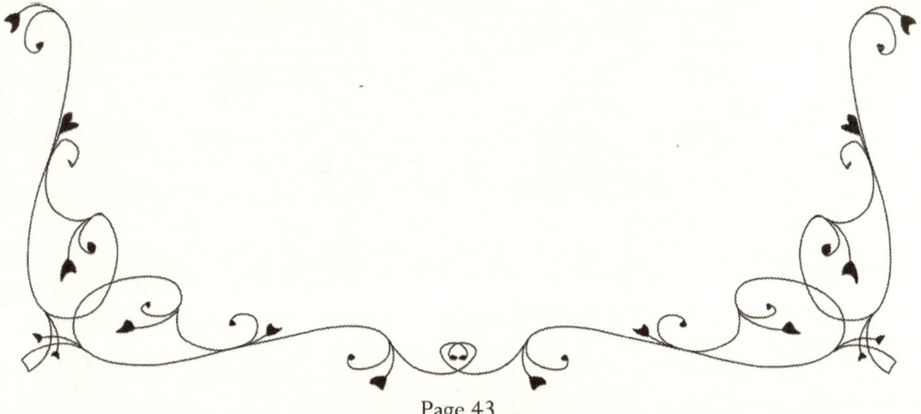

Notes

Mint Cucumber Tea Sandwiches

- 1 lg. tomato, chopped
- ½ c. fresh parsley, chopped
- ⅓ c. sliced green onion
- 2 cloves garlic, minced
- 1 T. lemon juice
- 1 T. olive oil
- ¼ t. pepper
- ¼ c. mint, chopped
- 2-3 cucumbers
- 1 8 oz. pkg. cream cheese softened
- ½ c. sour cream
- 1 loaf of dill rye bread or bread of choice
- butter

Beat cream cheese until smooth. Add remaining ingredients. Butter 1 slice of bread. Spread cream cheese mixture on slice. Chill before cutting. Cut each slice into four squares. Top with a cucumber slice. Sprinkle with pepper if desired. Makes about 32 tea sandwiches.

Notes

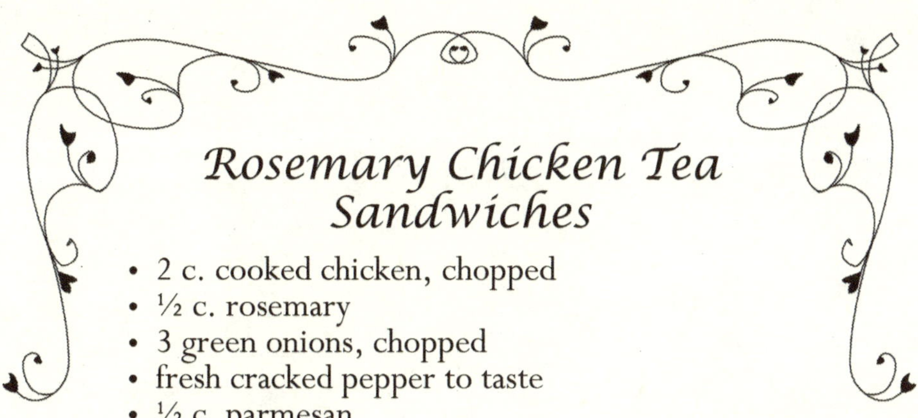

Rosemary Chicken Tea Sandwiches

- 2 c. cooked chicken, chopped
- ½ c. rosemary
- 3 green onions, chopped
- fresh cracked pepper to taste
- ½ c. parmesan
- 1 c. mayonnaise
- butter
- bread (potato bread, buttermilk bread, sourdough all work well)
- parsley for decoration

Mix together first five ingredients. Add just enough mayonnaise to bind mixture together – about 1 c. Spread butter on bread slices. Add filling and top with second slice. Cut into desired shapes – squares, triangles, etc. Sprinkle parsley on sides for decoration.

Notes

Cheddar Olive Tea Sandwiches

- 1 c. cheddar cheese
- ½ c. green olives
- 2 t. Worchestershire sauce
- 2 cloves garlic, minced
- ¼ c mayonnaise
- 1 8 oz. pkg. cream cheese
- ½ c. sour cream
- light rye bread
- butter

Beat cream cheese until smooth. Add remaining ingredients. Butter one slice of bread. Spread cream cheese mixture on slice. Chill before cutting. Cut each slice into squares. Top each with a slice of green olive. Makes about 32 tea sandwiches.

Notes

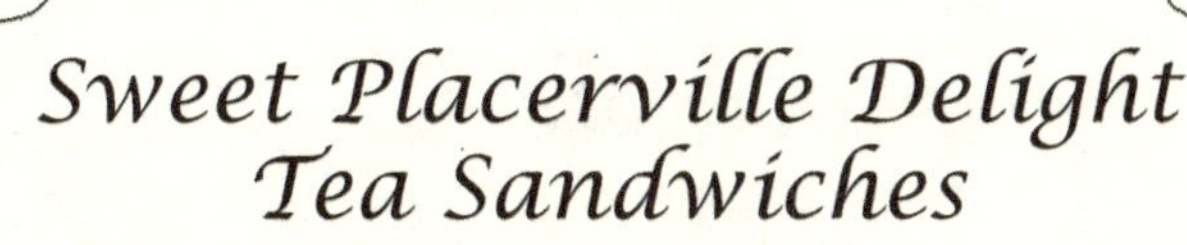

Sweet Placerville Delight Tea Sandwiches

- 1 Placer Sweet onion (Vidalia or Maui onion work well also)
- 1 T. butter
- 1 boullion cube – vegetable, beef or chicken
- ½ c. cream sherry
- 8 oz. cream cheese, softened
- butter
- bread (5 seed bread works well)

Preheat oven to 400°. Peel and cut a hole in the center of the onion, do not go all the way through (As if you would core it, but not all the way through). Place 1 T. butter and 1 boullion cube in the hole. Form a cup with a piece of foil. Place onion inside. Pour the cream sherry into the hole. Wrap up the onion completely. It will look like a Hershey's kiss when finished. Place on a pie plate and bake for 1½ hours. Cool. Save the onion juice.

Chop onion finely. Combine onion, juice and cream cheese. Spread butter on bread slices. Add onion filling and top with second slice. Cut into desired shapes-squares, triangles, etc. Enjoy!

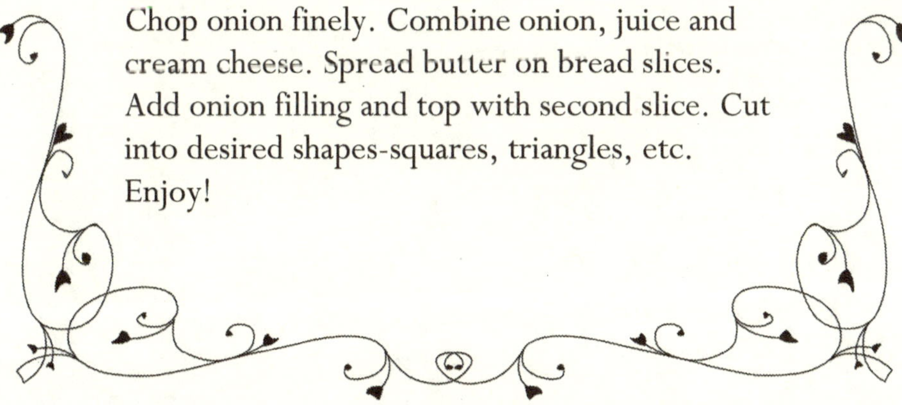

Notes

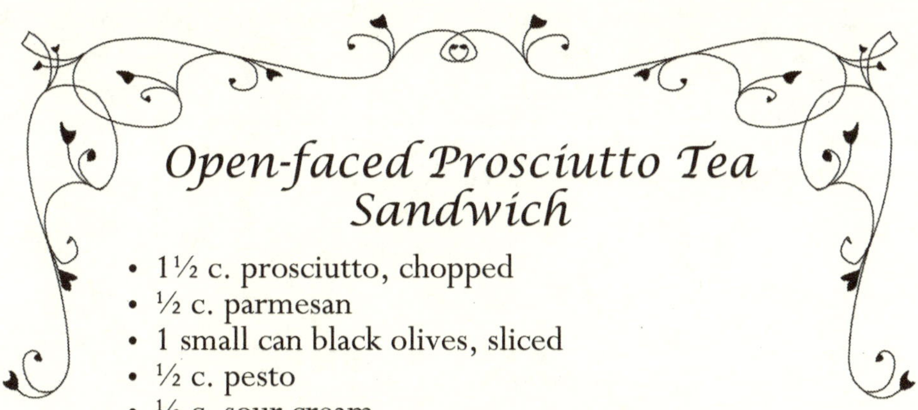

Open-faced Prosciutto Tea Sandwich

- 1½ c. prosciutto, chopped
- ½ c. parmesan
- 1 small can black olives, sliced
- ½ c. pesto
- ½ c. sour cream
- 1 8 oz. pkg. cream cheese, softened
- bread of choice, sliced thin

Beat cream cheese until smooth. Add prosciutto, parmesan, black olives and sour cream. Butter 1 slice of bread. Spread a thin layer of pesto on each slice. Spread a thin layer of cream cheese mixture on top. Chill before cutting. Cut each slice into squares. Top each with a slice of black olive.

Notes

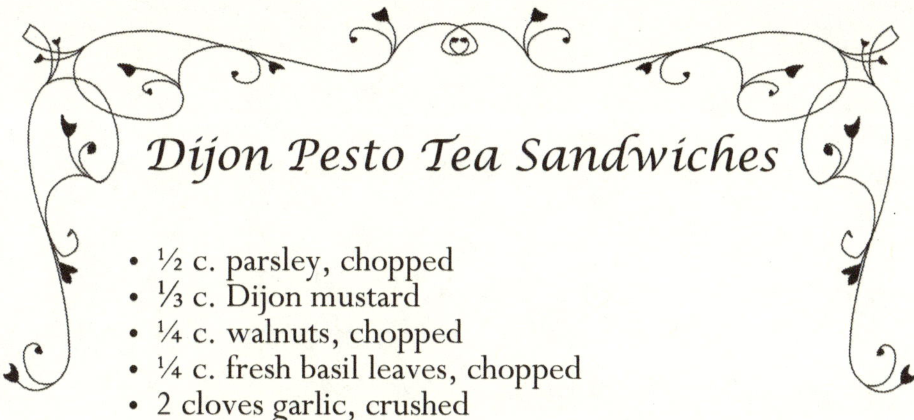

Dijon Pesto Tea Sandwiches

- ½ c. parsley, chopped
- ⅓ c. Dijon mustard
- ¼ c. walnuts, chopped
- ¼ c. fresh basil leaves, chopped
- 2 cloves garlic, crushed
- ¼ c. grated Parmesan cheese
- 1 8 oz. cream cheese, softened
- ½ c. sour cream
- seasoning salt for garnish
- small tomatoes, sliced – for garnish
- 1 loaf of 5 seed grain bread or bread of choice
- butter

Beat cream cheese until smooth. Add remaining ingredients except for seasoning salt and tomatoes. Butter 1 slice of bread. Spread cream cheese mixture on slice. Chill before cutting. Cut each slice into thirds. Top each with a slice of tomato. Sprinkle lightly with seasoning salt. Makes about 32 tea sandwiches.

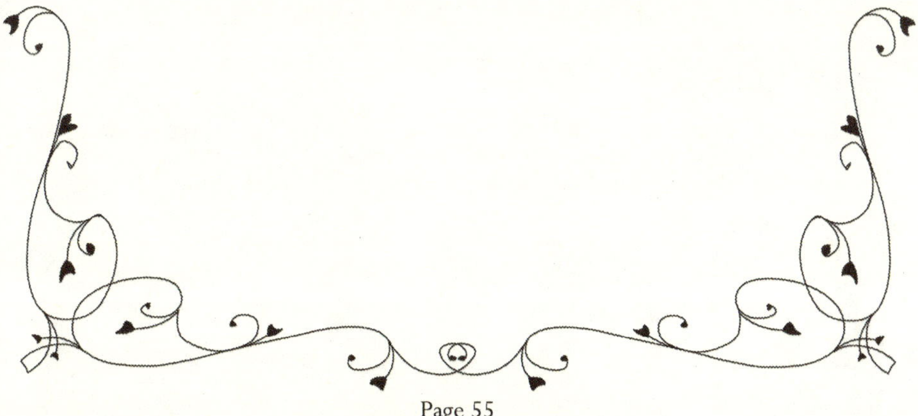

Notes

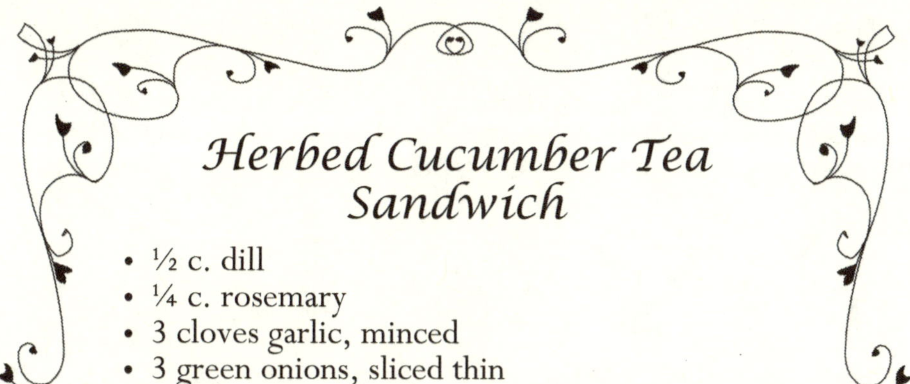

Herbed Cucumber Tea Sandwich

- ½ c. dill
- ¼ c. rosemary
- 3 cloves garlic, minced
- 3 green onions, sliced thin
- 1 8 oz. pkg. cream cheese, softened
- ½ c. sour cream
- 1 t. olive oil
- 2 cucumbers
- bread of choice, dill rye works very well
- butter

Beat cream cheese until smooth. Add remaining ingredients except for cucumbers. Butter 1 slice of bread. Spread cream cheese mixture on slice. Chill before cutting. Cut each slice into squares. Top each with a slice of cucumber. Makes about 32 tea sandwiches.

Notes

Savory Artichoke Cheesecake Tea Sandwiches

- 1 tablespoon butter or margarine, softened
- ¼ cup fine dry bread crumbs, divided
- 2 pkgs. (8 oz. each) cream cheese, softened
- 1 cup sour cream
- ¾ cup (4 oz.) crumbled feta cheese
- 3 large eggs
- 1 (9 oz.) pkg. frozen artichoke hearts, thawed
- 1 medium red pepper, chopped
- ½ cup sliced green onions
- 1 large clove garlic, crushed
- 1 teaspoon dried tarragon leaves, crushed
- ½ teaspoon dried basil leaves, crushed

To serve:

- optional garnish: fresh basil leaves, red pepper strips, cooked artichoke hearts
- rye and pumpernickel toast points or crackers

Preheat oven to 375°. With butter, grease inside of 9" springform pan. Sprinkle with bread crumbs to coat thickly; reserve remaining crumbs. Set pan aside.

In large bowl of electric mixer, at medium-high speed, beat cream cheese until fluffy. Add sour

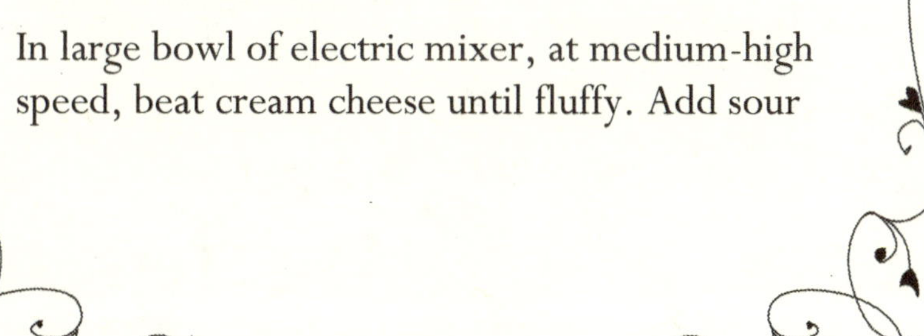

Notes

Savory Artichoke Cheesecake Tea Sandwiches Continued

cream, feta, and eggs; beat until blended and smooth.

Pat dry and finely chop artichoke hearts; add to bowl with cheese mixture. Beat in chopped pepper, onions, garlic, tarragon, and basil until blended. Spoon into prepared pan; spread evenly.

Bake 35 minutes, or until puffed and golden. Cool on wire rack to room temperature; refrigerate 3 hours or overnight.

To garnish and serve:

Remove springform side. Pat remaining bread crumbs onto side of cheesecake. If desired, garnish top of cheesecake with fresh basil leaves, red pepper strips and cooked artichoke hearts.

To serve, slice cheesecake in wedges; serve on toast points or crackers. Serves 24.

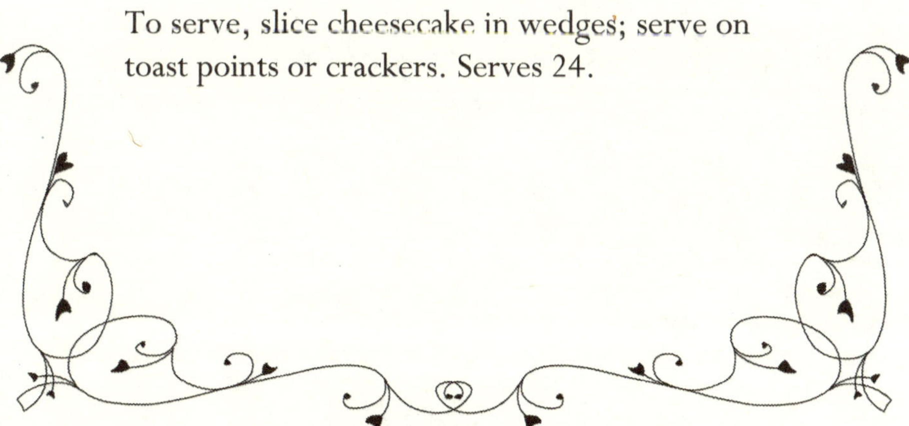

Notes

Italian Chicken Tea Sandwiches

- 2 c. cooked chicken, chopped
- 1 t. minced garlic
- ½ pkg of dry Italian Salad Dressing mix (Good Seasons)
- 3 green onions chopped – use white and green parts
- ¾ c mozzarella cheese, shredded
- ½ can (3 oz.) black olives, chopped
- 1 c. mayonnaise
- butter
- bread (potato bread, buttermilk bread, sourdough all work well)
- parsley for decoration

Mix together first six ingredients. Add just enough mayonnaise to bind mixture together – about 1 c. Spread butter on bread slices. Add filling and top with second slice. Cut into desired shapes-squares, triangles, etc. Sprinkle parsley on sides for decoration.

Notes

Roasted Red Pepper Tea Sandwiches (Open-faced)

- 2 T. sherry vinegar
- ⅓ c. fresh basil, chopped
- ¼ c. roasted red pepper
- 1 8 oz. pkg. cream cheese
- Lawry's seasoning salt to taste
- garlic powder to taste
- 1 loaf dark rye bread

Beat cream cheese until smooth. Add vinegar, basil, and red pepper. Butter 1 slice of bread. Spread cream cheese mixture on slice. Chill before cutting. Cut into each bread slice into 4 squares. Sprinkle with Lawry's seasoning and garlic powder to taste if desired. Makes about 32 tea sandwiches.

Note: We like to cut the dark rye first into rounds with a round cookie cutter and then spread the cream cheese mixture on each round. Then sprinkle with seasonings.

Notes

Desserts

Tropical Fruit Tea Cookie

Crust

- ¾ c. butter, softened
- ½ c. sugar
- 1 egg yolk
- ¼ t. lemon extract
- ½ t. vanilla
- 2 c. flour
- ¼ c. finely chopped walnuts

Topping

- 1¼ c. nuts, chopped
- 2 c. chopped dried fruit including dried cherries, dried apricots, dried cranberries, dried pineapple
- 2 T. lightly salted butter
- 3 T. superfine sugar
- 1 T. milk
- 2 t. vanilla

In mixing bowl, cream butter and sugar. Beat in the egg yolk, lemon extract and vanilla. Gradually add in flour and nuts. Form into 2 logs. Wrap in plastic wrap. Chill overnight. Preheat oven to 400°. Slice about ¼ inch thick and then place on an ungreased cookie sheet

Notes

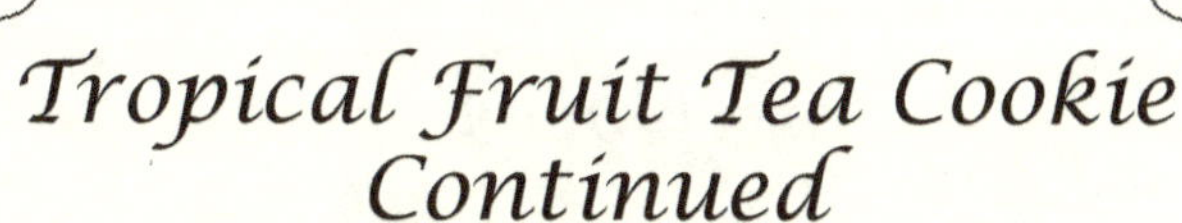

Tropical Fruit Tea Cookie Continued

about 2 inches apart. Bake for 3-4 minutes just to firm them up a bit.

For topping:

Place 2 T. butter, superfine sugar, milk and vanilla in a heavy-bottomed saucepan and heat gently to dissolve. Try to avoid stirring too much. Add the nuts and leave to cool. Stir in the fruit. Top each cookie with mixture and bake for another 3-4 minutes. Gently remove from pan. This is a delicate cookie.

Notes

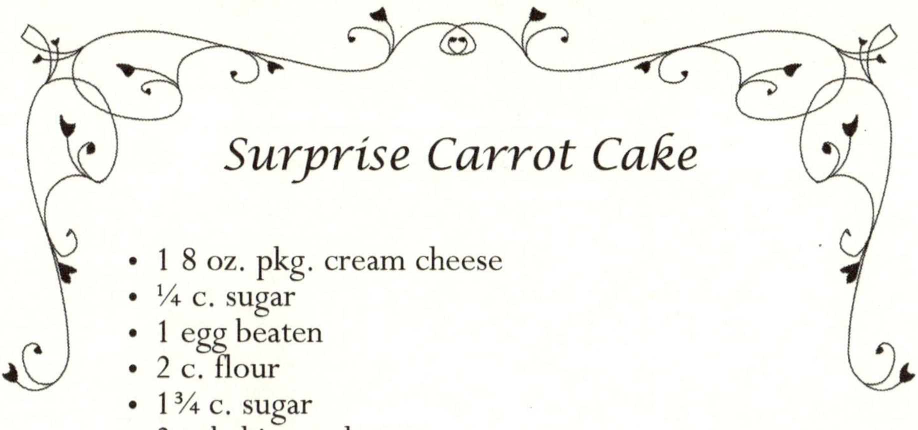

Surprise Carrot Cake

- 1 8 oz. pkg. cream cheese
- ¼ c. sugar
- 1 egg beaten
- 2 c. flour
- 1¾ c. sugar
- 2 t. baking soda
- 2 t. cinnamon
- 1 t. salt
- 1 c. oil
- 3 eggs, beaten
- 3 c. shredded carrot
- ½ c. nuts, chopped

Frosting

- 1 3 oz. pkg. cream cheese, softened
- ¼ c. butter, softened
- 2 c. powdered sugar
- whipping cream or milk to thin frosting

Preheat oven to 350°. Brush large Bundt pan with shortening. Combine cream cheese, sugar and egg, mixing until well blended. Set aside.

Combine dry ingredients. Add combined oil and

Notes

Surprise Carrot Cake Continued

eggs, mixing just until moistened. Fold in carrots and nuts. Reserve 2 c. batter; pour remaining batter into greased and floured 9 inch Bundt pan. Pour cream cheese mixture over batter; carefully spoon reserved batter over cream cheese mixture, spreading to cover. Bake at 350° for 55 minutes. Cool 10 minutes; remove from pan. Cool thoroughly.

Frosting: Beat together cream cheese and butter until fluffy. Gradually add powdered sugar, beating until smooth. Add enough whipping cream or milk to thin to desired consistency. For the large Bundt cake we like to thin the frosting into a glaze.

Glaze cake with frosting. Makes 12 servings.

You can use mini Bundt pans with this recipe. Make sure you brush shortening in the mold first. On the little cakes we like to pipe the frosting on each cake. Makes about 36 mini Bundts.

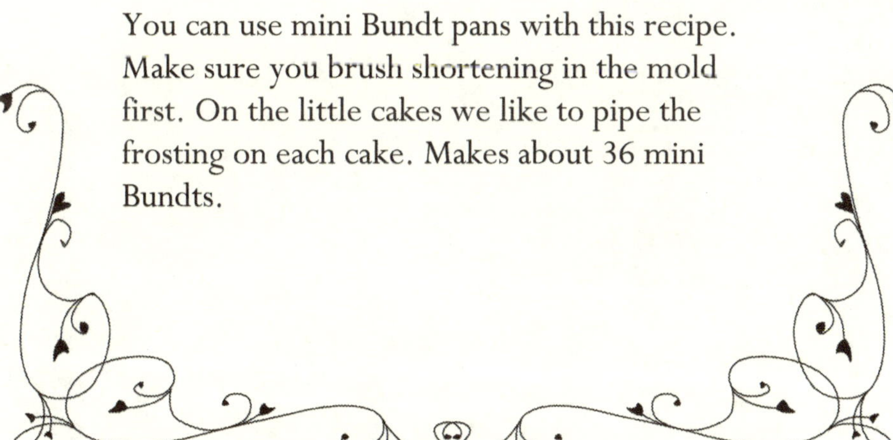

Notes

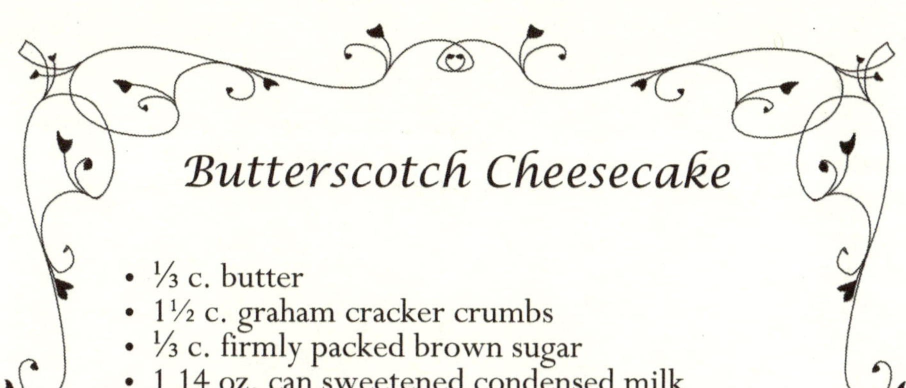

Butterscotch Cheesecake

- ⅓ c. butter
- 1½ c. graham cracker crumbs
- ⅓ c. firmly packed brown sugar
- 1 14 oz. can sweetened condensed milk
- ¾ c. cold water
- 1 pkg. butterscotch pudding and pie filling mix (not instant)
- 3 8 oz. pkg. cream cheese, softened
- 3 eggs
- 1 t. vanilla extract
- whipped cream
- crushed hard butterscotch candy

Preheat oven to 375°. Combine butter, crumbs and sugar; press firmly on bottom of 9"x9" pan. In medium saucepan, combine sweetened condensed milk and water; mix well. Stir in pudding mix. Over medium heat, cook and stir until thickened and bubbly. In large mixer bowl, beat cream cheese until fluffy. Beat in eggs and vanilla then pudding mixture. Pour into prepared pan. Bake 50 minutes or until golden brown around edge (center will be soft). Cool to room temperature. Chill thoroughly. Cut into squares and place in small glass dishes. Garnish with whipped cream and crushed candy.

Notes

Sugar and Spice Pecans

- 1 c. sugar
- 2 t. fresh orange zest
- 1 t. cinnamon
- ¼ t. salt
- ½ t. ground ginger
- 2 egg whites
- ¼ ground nutmeg
- ¼ c. melted butter
- ¼ ground allspice
- 4 c. pecan halves

Stir together sugar, spices, orange zest and salt. Beat egg whites at high speed with an electric mixer until foamy. Gradually add sugar mixture, beating at high speed until soft peaks form. Fold in melted butter and pecan halves. Spread coated nuts in a single layer on a large cookie sheet lined with nonstick aluminum foil or parchment paper.

Bake at 250° for 45 minutes or until nuts are toasted, stirring every 15 minutes. Remove from oven; let cool completely on pan. Store in an airtight container up to 2 weeks.

Makes 4 cups.

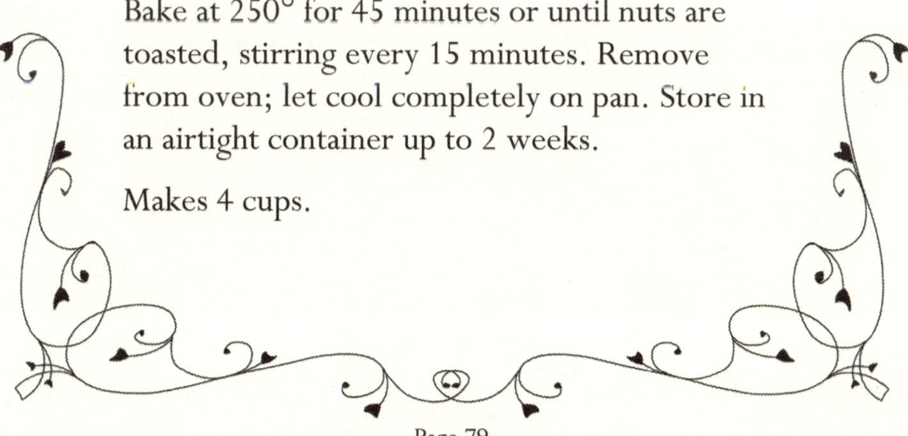

Notes

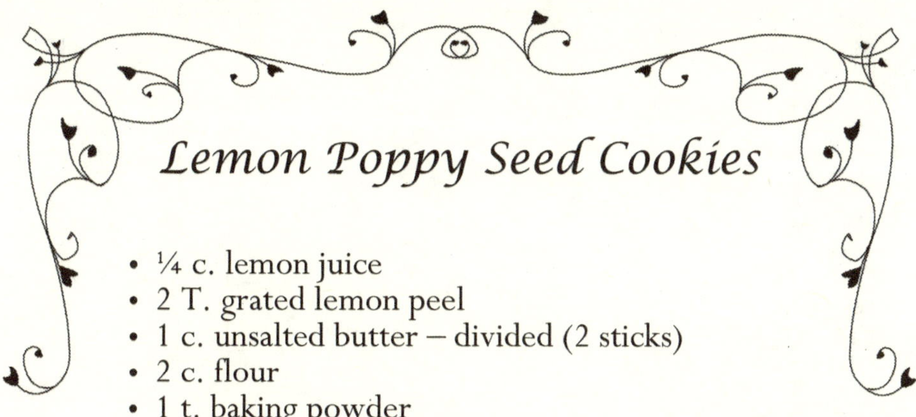

Lemon Poppy Seed Cookies

- ¼ c. lemon juice
- 2 T. grated lemon peel
- 1 c. unsalted butter – divided (2 sticks)
- 2 c. flour
- 1 t. baking powder
- ½ t. salt
- 1½ c. sugar – divided
- 1 egg
- 2 t. vanilla extract
- 1 T. poppy seeds plus additional seeds for decoration

Preheat oven to 375°. Bring lemon juice to a simmer in a small saucepan over medium heat; cook until reduced by half. Add 1 stick of butter; stir until melted.

Mix flour, baking powder and salt. Cream remaining stick of butter and 1 c. sugar on medium speed of mixer. Mix in egg and lemon butter for about 3 minutes. Stir in vanilla and 1 T. lemon peel. Mix in flour mixture and poppy seeds.

Stir together remaining ½ c. sugar and

Notes

Lemon Poppy Seed Cookies Continued

remaining 1 T. lemon peel. Form the dough into balls; roll them in the sugar mixture. Place about 2 inches apart on baking sheets. Flatten with a glass dipped in sugar mixture until ¼" thick. Sprinkle with seeds.

Bake about 10-12 minutes. Cool on wire racks. Store in an airtight container.

Notes

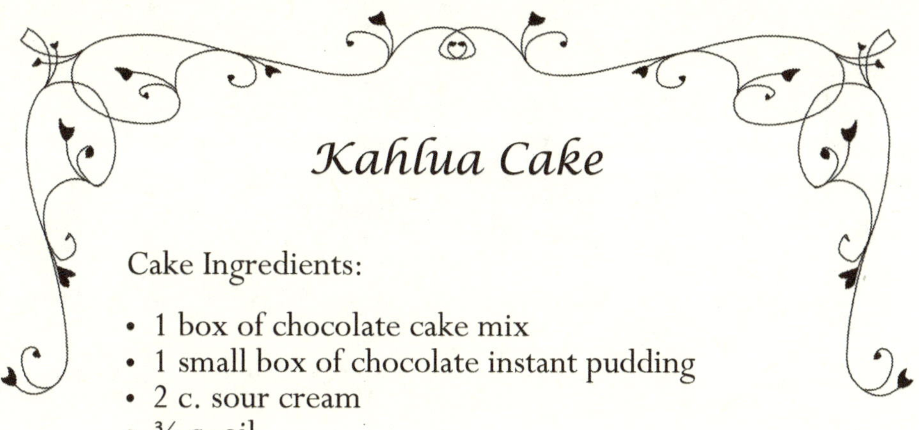

Kahlua Cake

Cake Ingredients:

- 1 box of chocolate cake mix
- 1 small box of chocolate instant pudding
- 2 c. sour cream
- ¾ c. oil
- 3 eggs
- 1 c. chocolate chips
- ⅓ c. kahlua
- 1 t. vanilla

Glaze:

- ½ c. cocoa
- 2 c. powdered sugar
- water – enough to make desired consistency

Preheat oven 350°. Spray large Bundt pan with Pam. Combine cake ingredients in a large bowl. Beat with electric mixer for about 2 minutes. Pour batter into pan. Bake at 350° for about 40-60 minutes or until a knife comes out clean when inserted into the cake. Cool.

Combine glaze ingredients. Add enough water to make desired consistency. Spoon glaze over

Notes

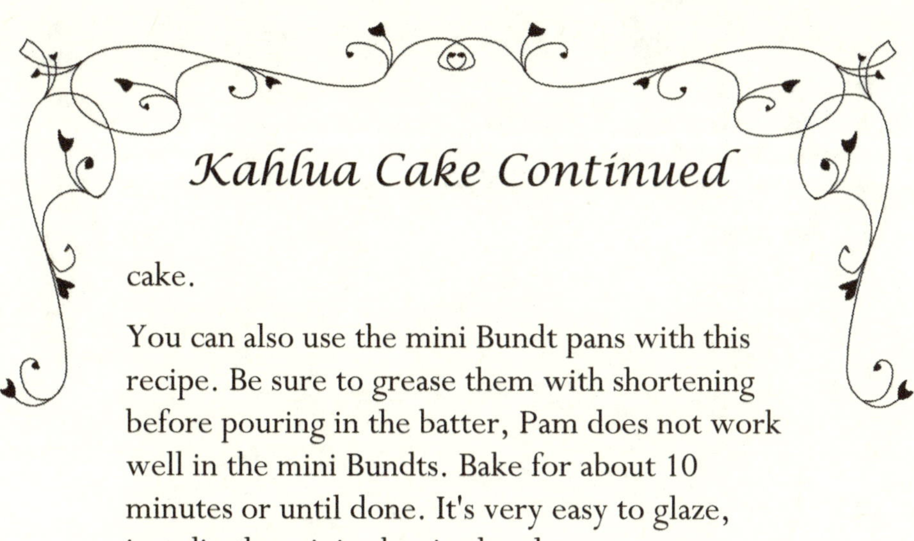

Kahlua Cake Continued

cake.

You can also use the mini Bundt pans with this recipe. Be sure to grease them with shortening before pouring in the batter, Pam does not work well in the mini Bundts. Bake for about 10 minutes or until done. It's very easy to glaze, just dip the mini cakes in the glaze.

Notes

Cappuccino Brownies

Brownie

- 1 pkg brownie mix
- 1 T. instant coffee or more to taste dissolved in 1 T. water

Cappuccino Frosting

- 1 1b. box of powdered sugar
- ½ c. butter-softened
- 1 t. vanilla
- 1 T. instant coffee dissolved in 1-2 T. water
- chocolate chips for decoration (white or dark)

For brownies, follow directions according to package and add in instant coffee mixture. Cool completely. Cut into squares. Pipe a small rosette on each brownie with Cappuccino Frosting. For garnish add a chocolate chip (white or brown) in the center of each rosette.

Notes

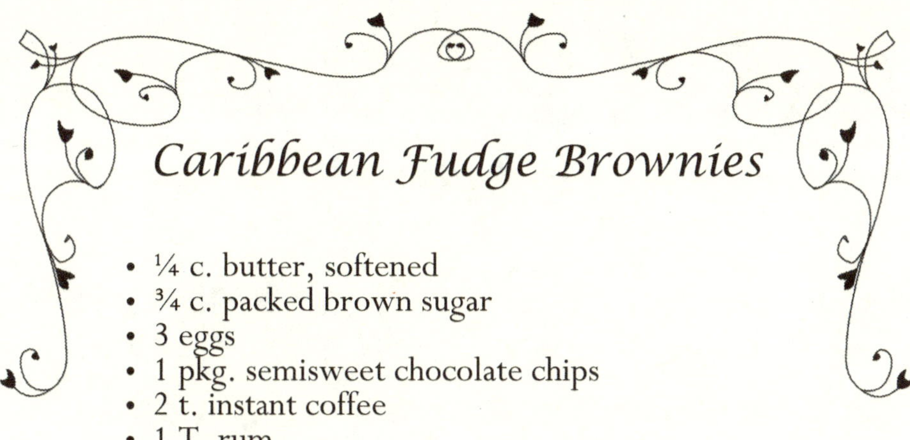

Caribbean Fudge Brownies

- ¼ c. butter, softened
- ¾ c. packed brown sugar
- 3 eggs
- 1 pkg. semisweet chocolate chips
- 2 t. instant coffee
- 1 T. rum
- ¼ c. flour
- 1 c. walnuts, chopped
- ½ c. walnut halves
- powdered sugar or whipped cream for garnish if desired

Preheat oven to 375°. Spray a 9"x9" pan with Pam. In a large bowl cream butter and brown sugar. Add eggs, one at a time, beating well after each addition. Melt chocolate chips in separate bowl in the microwave at ½ power until melted. Add to creamed mixture with coffee and rum. Stir in flour and the 1 c. walnuts. Pour into pan and decorate top with the ½ c. walnut halves. Bake at 375° for 20 minutes or until knife inserted near center comes out clean. Cool on wire rack. Store in refrigerator-covered. Garnish with powdered sugar or whipped cream if desired. This recipe freezes very well.

Notes

Sherry Tea Cakes

Cake ingredients:

- 1 box yellow cake mix
- 1 box instant vanilla pudding
- ¾ c. cream sherry
- ¾ c. oil
- 4 eggs
- ¾ t. nutmeg

Glaze:

- 4 c. powdered sugar
- ½ c. cream sherry

Preheat oven to 350°. Brush pans with shortening. Do not use Pam. Mix the cake ingredients above in a large bowl. Beat with electric mixer for 2 minutes.

Pour batter into small Bundt pans and bake until done about 6-10 minutes or until toothpick comes out clean when inserted into cake.

For the glaze: mix powdered sugar and ½ c. cream sherry together. Beat until creamy. Drizzle glaze over cooled cakes or dip cooled cakes into glaze. Makes approximately 24 tea cakes.

Notes

Chocolate Crinkles

- 1 c. chocolate chips
- 1 c. flour
- 1 c. brown sugar
- 1 t. baking powder
- ⅓ c. oil
- ½ t. salt
- 2 eggs
- ½ c. chopped nuts
- 1 t. vanilla
- ½ c. powdered sugar

Place chips in microwave on high for 2 minutes. Blend in brown sugar and oil. Add eggs, 1 at a time beating well. Stir in vanilla. Combine flour, baking powder and salt; stir into chocolate. Mix in nuts. Chill at least 1 hour. Do not freeze dough.

Preheat oven 350°. Form dough into balls and roll in powdered sugar. Bake for 5-6 minutes.

Notes

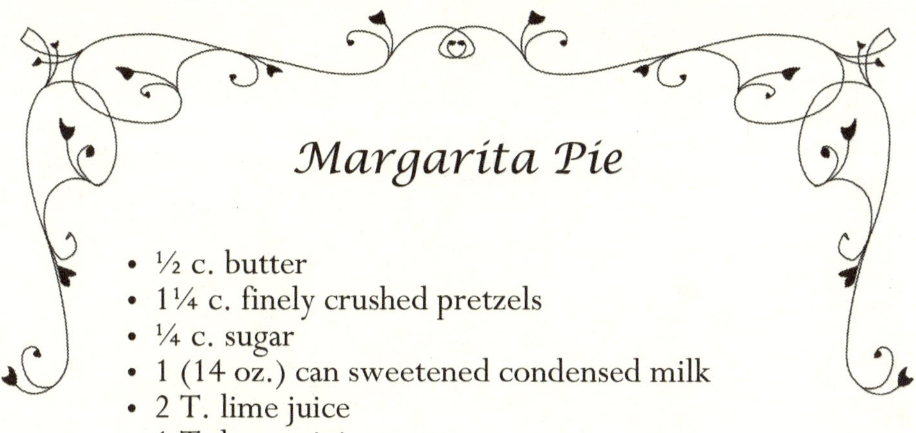

Margarita Pie

- ½ c. butter
- 1¼ c. finely crushed pretzels
- ¼ c. sugar
- 1 (14 oz.) can sweetened condensed milk
- 2 T. lime juice
- 1 T. lemon juice
- 3 T. tequila
- 3 T. triple sec
- 1 c. whipping cream – whipped in a separate bowl until very stiff
- additional whipping cream for garnish
- slices of fresh lime for garnish

In small bowl melt butter in the microwave. Stir in pretzel crumbs and sugar. Mix well. Press crumbs on bottom of 9"x9" pan. Chill.

In large bowl, combine sweetened condensed milk, lime juice, lemon juice, tequila, and triple sec; mix well. Fold in whipped cream. Pour into crust. Freeze until firm overnight in freezer. Cut into squares and place in small glass dishes. Garnish with additional whipped cream and a slice of lime. Makes 16-20 tea desserts.

Notes

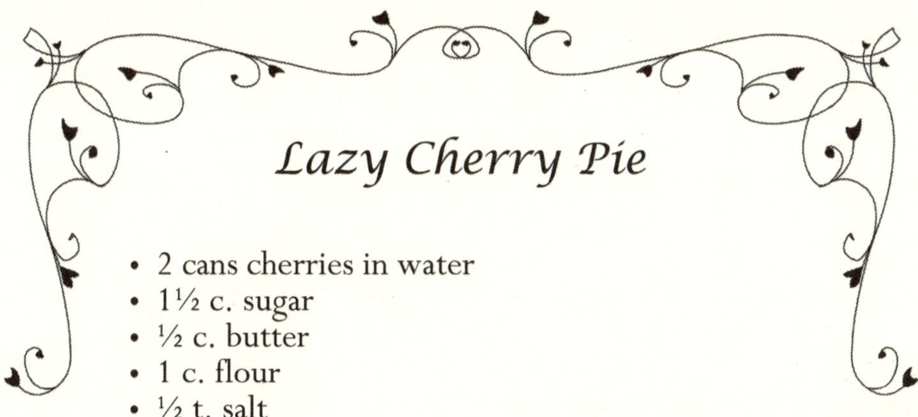

Lazy Cherry Pie

- 2 cans cherries in water
- 1½ c. sugar
- ½ c. butter
- 1 c. flour
- ½ t. salt
- ¾ c. milk
- 2 t. baking powder

Melt butter in a 9"x13" inch pan while preheating oven to 350°. Sift sugar, flour and salt in bowl. Mix in milk. Pour batter into butter. Add cherries. Do Not Mix! Sprinkle with sugar.

Bake at 350° for 1 hour until brown and is set.

Notes

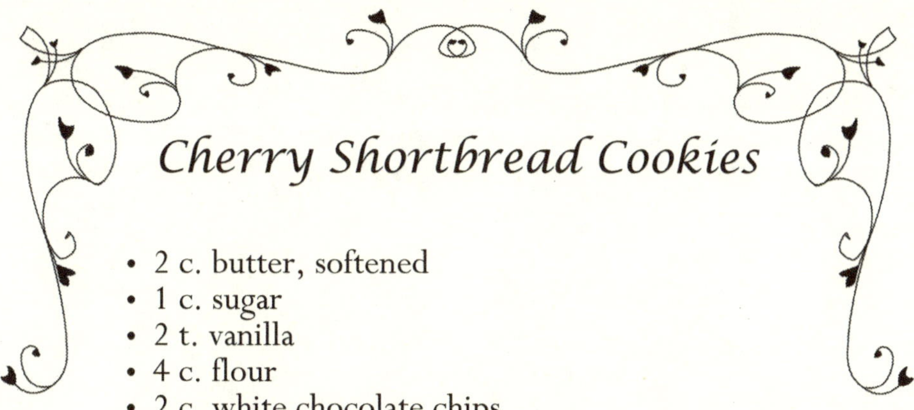

Cherry Shortbread Cookies

- 2 c. butter, softened
- 1 c. sugar
- 2 t. vanilla
- 4 c. flour
- 2 c. white chocolate chips
- 1½ c. dried cherries

Preheat oven to 350°. Beat butter, sugar and vanilla in a large bowl with electric mixer on medium speed until light and fluffy. Add flour; mix well.

Stir in 1 c. chocolate chips and cherries. Drop rounded tablespoons of dough, 2 inches apart onto ungreased cookie sheet. Flatten each ball of dough slightly.

Bake 10-14 minutes or until lightly browned. Cool 5 minutes on baking sheets. Remove to wire racks; cool completely.

In a small bowl, melt 1 c. white chocolate chips in the microwave until melted. Dip half of each cookie into melted white chocolate. Allow to dry before serving.

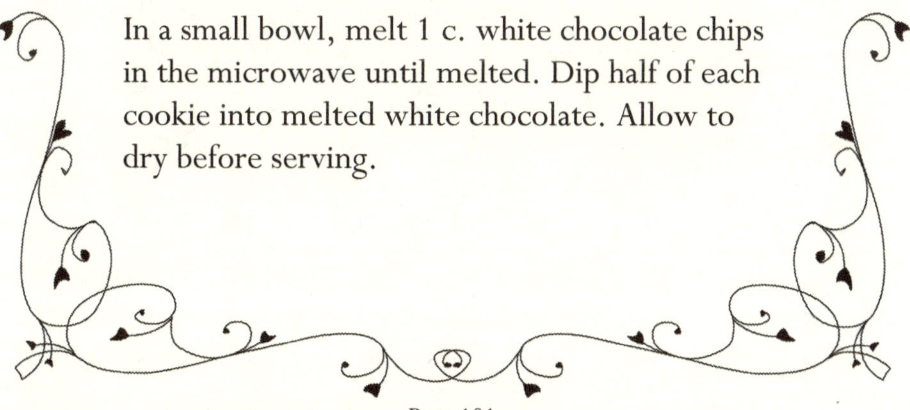

Notes

Lemon Tea Cookies

This recipe was submitted by Marge Benson, a recipe contest winner from our 2005 Anniversary party. We adapted it a bit for our tearoom.

Crust

- ¾ c. butter, softened
- ½ c. sugar
- 1 egg yolk
- ½ t. vanilla
- ½ t. lemon extract
- 2 c. flour
- ¼ c. finely chopped walnuts

Filling

- 3 T. butter, softened
- 4½ t. lemon juice
- ¾ t. grated orange peel
- ¾ t. grated lemon peel
- 1½ c. powdered sugar

In mixing bowl, cream butter and sugar. Beat in the egg yolk, lemon extract and vanilla. Gradually add in flour. Form into two 14 inch

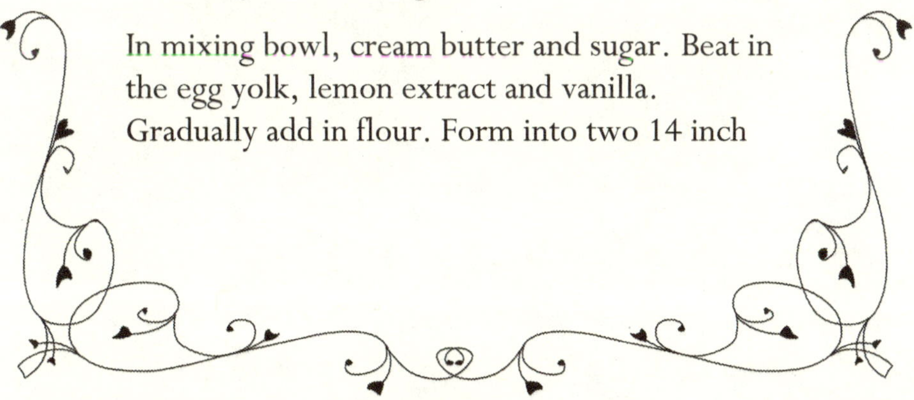

Notes

Lemon Tea Cookies Continued

logs. Reshape each roll into a 14" x 1 ⅛" x 1 ⅛" block. Wrap each in plastic wrap. Chill overnight. Cut into about ¼" thick slices and then place on an ungreased cookie sheet about 2 inches apart. Sprinkle half of the cookies with nuts, gently pressing onto dough. Bake at 400° for 8-10 minutes or until golden brown around the edges. Remove to wire racks to cool.

In a small mixing bowl, cream butter, lemon juice, orange and lemon peel. Gradually add powdered sugar. Spread about 1 t. on bottom of the plain cookies; place nut topped cookies over filling. Makes about 4½ dozen.

Notes

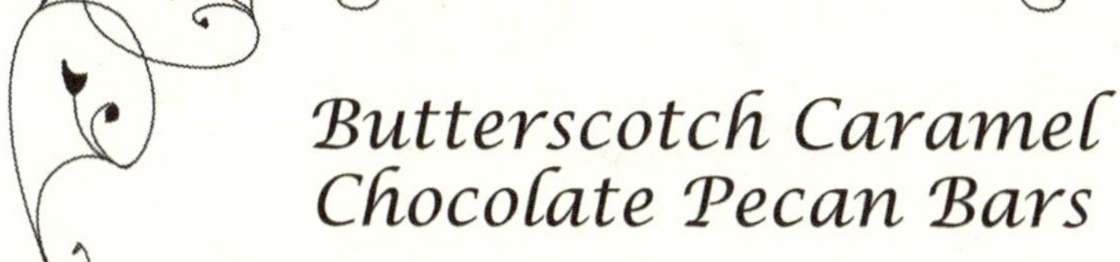

Butterscotch Caramel Chocolate Pecan Bars

Crust

- 2 c. flour
- 1 c. brown sugar
- ½ c. butter, softened
- 1 c. pecans

Filling

- ⅔ c. butter
- ½ c. brown sugar
- 1 c. butterscotch chips
- 1 c. chocolate chips

Preheat oven to 350°.

To make crust: combine flour, 1 c. brown sugar and ½ c. butter. Beat at medium speed until well mixed about 3 minutes. Press on bottom of an ungreased 9"x13" pan. Sprinkle pecans over unbaked crust.

For filling: Combine ⅔ c. butter and ½ c. brown sugar in a medium saucepan. Cook over medium heat, stirring constantly until mixture comes to a full boil. Cook 1 minute more. Pour

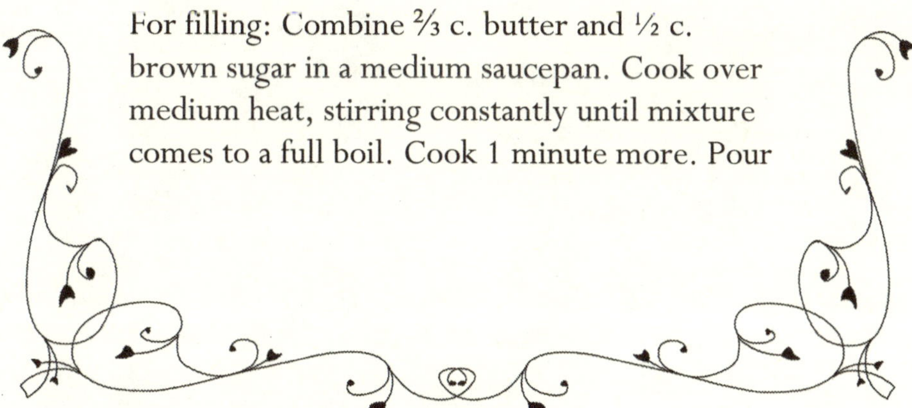

Notes

Butterscotch Caramel Chocolate Pecan Bars Continued

over pecans and crust. Bake for 18-20 minutes or until entire caramel layer is bubbly. Immediately sprinkle butterscotch and chocolate chips over caramel layer. Swirl chips leaving some whole for a marbled effect. Cool completely; cut into bars. Makes about 3 dozen bars.

Notes

Scones and Condiments

Tips on Making Scones

Use quality ingredients.

Use cold butter, don't let it soften-cold butter makes the scones rise higher.

Drain fruit very well.

Add fruit last, barely mix it in to flour mixture.

Add only enough buttermilk to make dough stick together.

If dough is too sticky when you pat it on the floured board, add more flour.

If dough is too dry and crumbles when you try and pat it on the floured board, add more buttermilk.

If you are using frozen fruit, make sure it does not thaw out. Mix it in quickly and cut scones fast. If it thaws out, the dough is very sticky and a mess!

Make sure oven is hot and preheated to 400°.

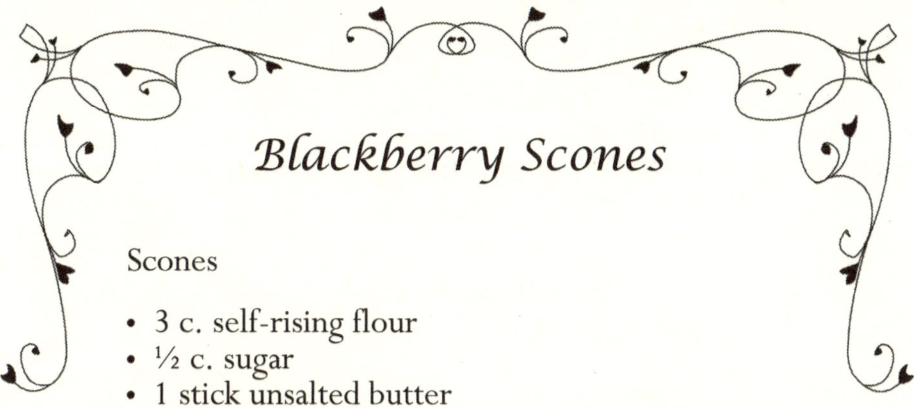

Blackberry Scones

Scones

- 3 c. self-rising flour
- ½ c. sugar
- 1 stick unsalted butter
- 1 c. buttermilk
- ½ c. blackberries

Glaze

- 1 c. powdered sugar
- 2-3 T. water

Combine flour and sugar. Cut in butter until mixture is coarse and crumbly. Add blackberries. Add just enough buttermilk to make a soft dough. Turn out on a floured board and cut with a biscuit or cookie cutter.

Place scones close together on a cookie sheet sprayed with vegetable oil. Bake at 400° until lightly browned about 10 minutes. Brush with glaze while still hot. Enjoy!

Notes

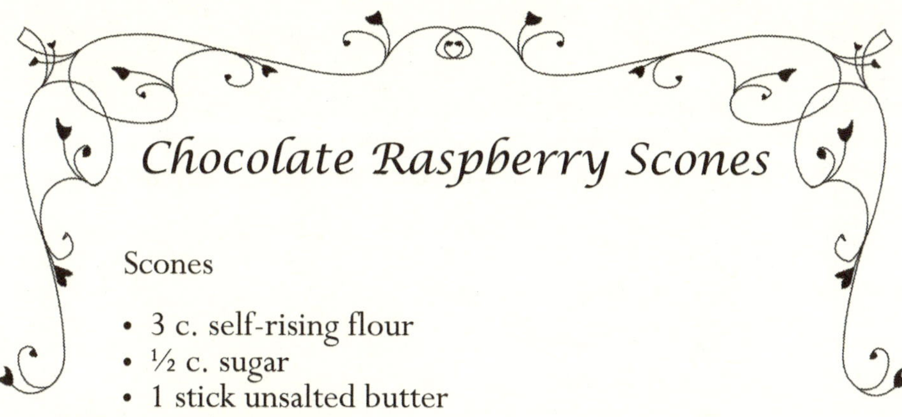

Chocolate Raspberry Scones

Scones

- 3 c. self-rising flour
- ½ c. sugar
- 1 stick unsalted butter
- 1 c. buttermilk
- ½ c. raspberries
- ½ c. semisweeet chocolate chips

Glaze

- 1 cup powdered sugar
- 2-3 tablespoons water

Combine flour and sugar. Cut in butter until mixture is coarse and crumbly. Add chocolate chips. Carefully fold in raspberries. Add just enough buttermilk to make a soft dough. Turn out on a floured board and cut with a biscuit or cookie cutter.

Place scones close together on a cookie sheet sprayed with vegetable oil. Bake at 400° until lightly browned about 10-25 minutes depending on your oven. Brush with glaze while still hot. Enjoy!

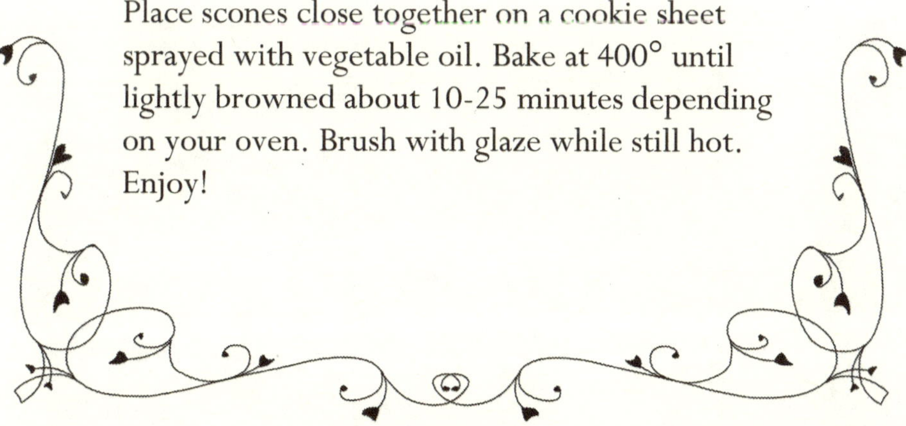

Notes

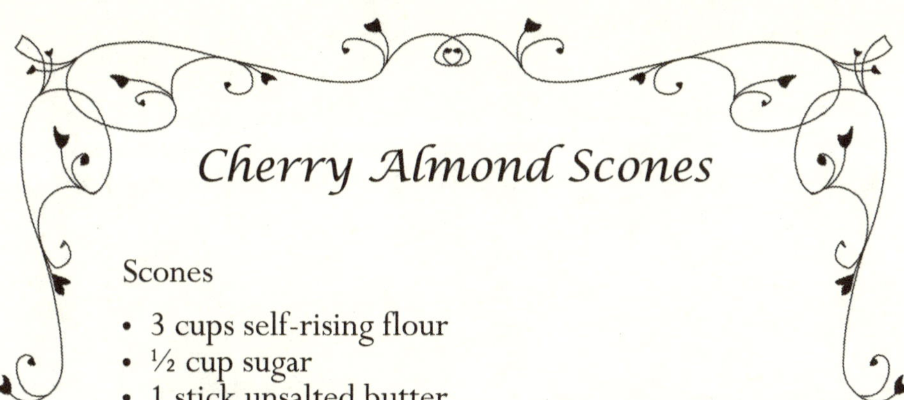

Cherry Almond Scones

Scones

- 3 cups self-rising flour
- ½ cup sugar
- 1 stick unsalted butter
- 1 cup buttermilk
- 1 cup dried cherries
- 1 t. almond extract
- ½ c. almonds

Glaze

- 1 cup powdered sugar
- 2-3 tablespoons water

Combine flour and sugar. Cut in butter until mixture is coarse and crumbly. Add dried cherries and almonds. Add almond extract to buttermilk. Add just enough of buttermilk mixture to make a soft dough. Turn out on a floured board and cut with a biscuit or cookie cutter.

Place scones close together on a cookie sheet sprayed with vegetable oil. Bake at 400° until lightly browned about 10 minutes. Brush with glaze while still hot. Sprinkle with almonds. Enjoy!

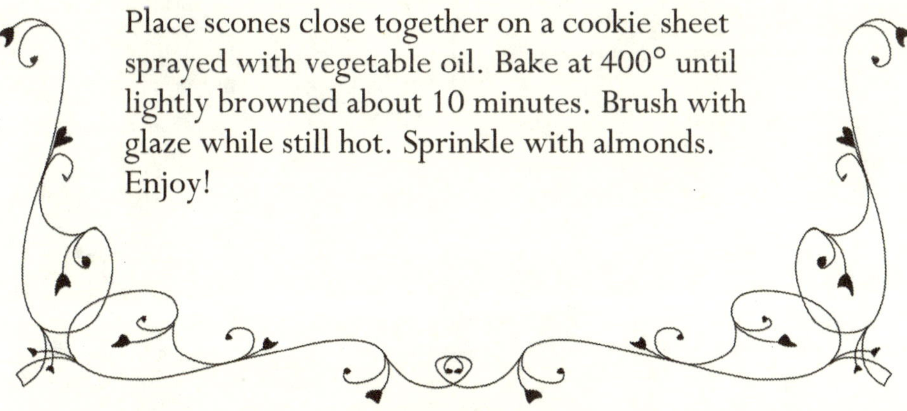

Notes

Lemon Curd

- ½ c. butter
- 1 c. granulated sugar
- ½ c. lemon juice
- 1½ t. grated lemon zest
- 3 eggs

Melt butter in microwave for 1 minute. Beat eggs in a glass bowl with an electric mixer until frothy. Mix in butter, sugar, lemon juice and zest. Microwave on HIGH for 3 minutes.

Beat mixture again until smooth. Microwave on HIGH for another 3 minutes. Beat mixture again until smooth. Refrigerate until set/cool. Lemon curd will keep up to 2 weeks in refrigerator.

Makes about 1 cup of lemon curd.

Notes

Devonshire Cream

This is not a "true" Devonshire cream, but our customers love our version.

- 1 8 oz. pkg. softened cream cheese
- 2 c. powdered sugar
- ½ freshly squeezed lemon
- 2 t. vanilla
- 1 c. sour cream

In a small bowl with an electric mixer, beat cream cheese, lemon juice, and vanilla. Gradually beat in powdered sugar. Fold in sour cream.

Makes 1½ cups.

Notes

Index

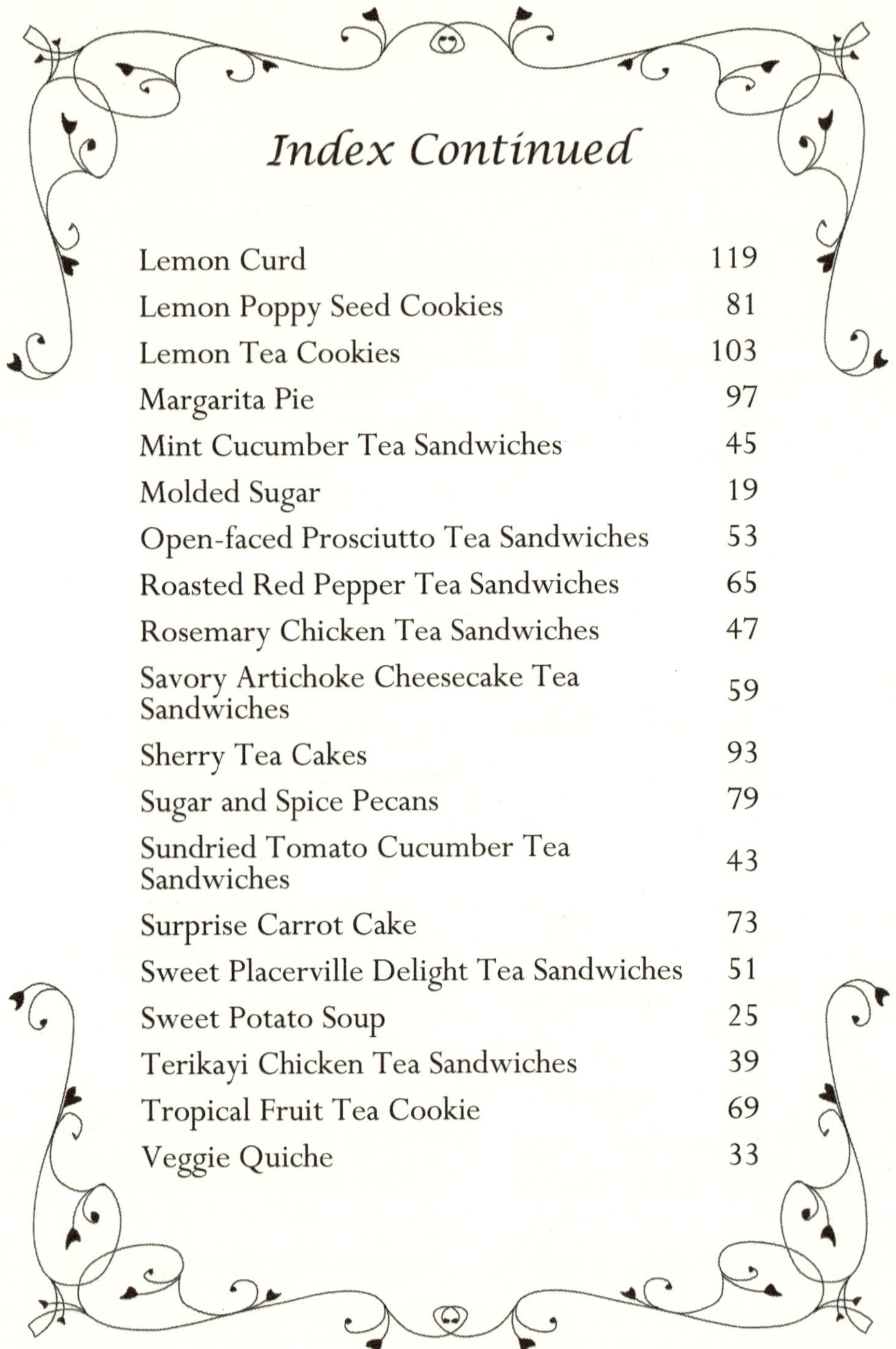

Index Continued

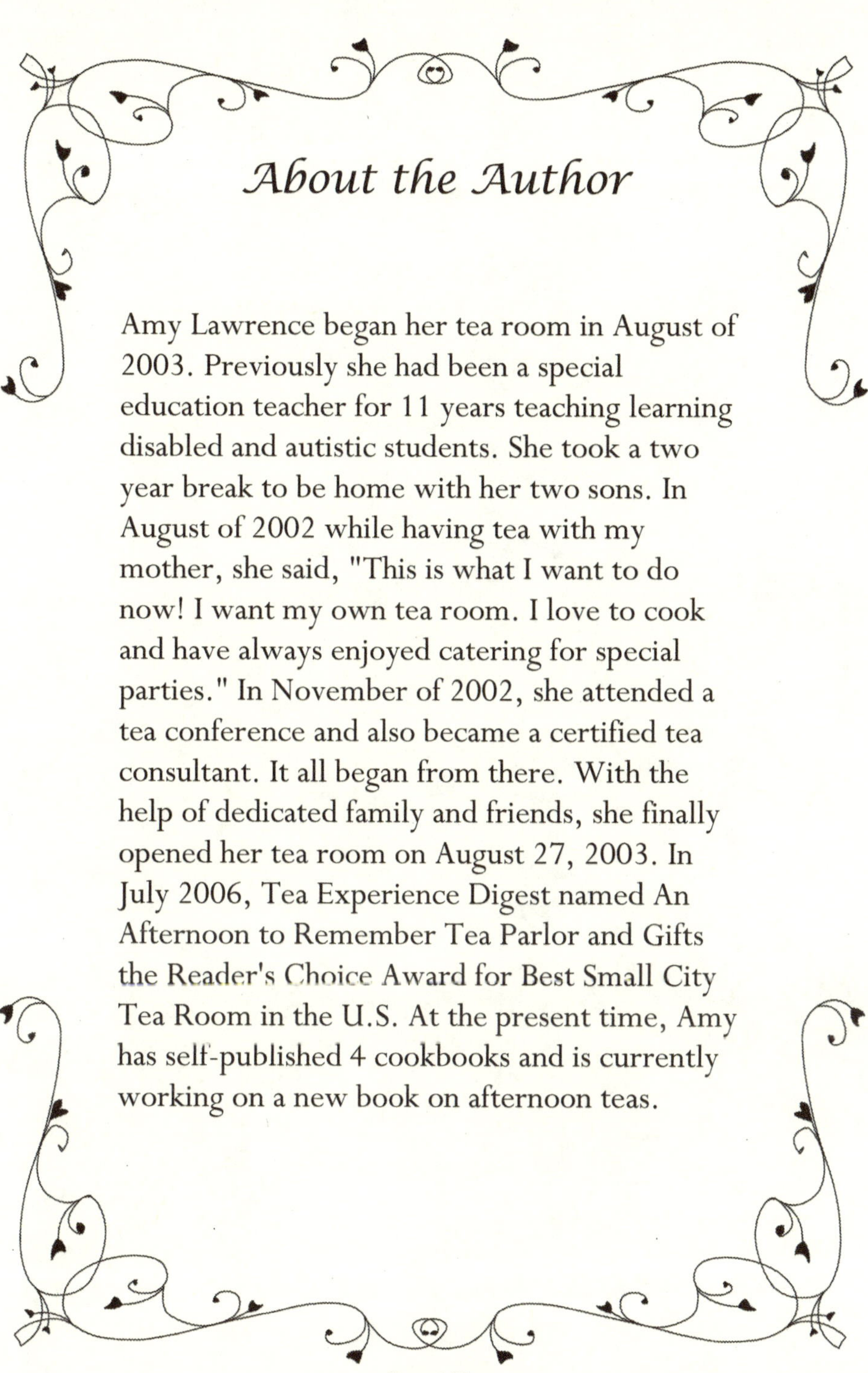

About the Author

Amy Lawrence began her tea room in August of 2003. Previously she had been a special education teacher for 11 years teaching learning disabled and autistic students. She took a two year break to be home with her two sons. In August of 2002 while having tea with my mother, she said, "This is what I want to do now! I want my own tea room. I love to cook and have always enjoyed catering for special parties." In November of 2002, she attended a tea conference and also became a certified tea consultant. It all began from there. With the help of dedicated family and friends, she finally opened her tea room on August 27, 2003. In July 2006, Tea Experience Digest named An Afternoon to Remember Tea Parlor and Gifts the Reader's Choice Award for Best Small City Tea Room in the U.S. At the present time, Amy has self-published 4 cookbooks and is currently working on a new book on afternoon teas.

www.ingramcontent.com/pod-product-compliance
Lightning Source LLC
LaVergne TN
LVHW091007080826
845145LV00003B/1166

* 9 7 8 0 9 7 9 6 1 7 0 2 7 *